Little Lessons to Live By

Little Lessons to Live By

E. Charles Bauer

Concordia Publishing House
St. Louis   London

Concordia Publishing House, St. Louis, Missouri
Concordia Publishing House Ltd., London, E. C. 1
Copyright © 1972 by Concordia Publishing House
Library of Congress Catalog Card No. 79-175143
International Standard Book No. ISBN-0570-03131-1

CONTENTS

Author's Preface

These little lessons were originally presented to little people. However, the response of the more mature people who "listened in" was such that it was decided to make them available to all who, in some way, might profit from them.

The language and the ideas embodied in these talks are suited to the mental level of the child. Maybe he can read them himself. Or they can be read to him. And, of course, they can be "preached" to him — the child. But the greatest Preacher of all time warned that unless we become as little children we have little chance of entering into the kingdom of heaven. Perhaps, then, it should not be surprising if in these days of intellectual sophistication these simple sermons, with a little embellishment, appeal to the sincere Christian of any age.

Moreover, these are not only *simple* sermons, but sample sermons too. No preacher preaches successfully unless he preaches himself. In view of the current demand for material of this kind, it is hoped that these simple samples may be the seed of much more fruitful homilies as a result of the personal touch of preachers more eloquent than

THE AUTHOR

Publisher's Preface

The need for fresh and relevant expositions of the Scriptures to children wells anew continually. It is a special satisfaction therefore to be able to offer to worship leaders these pretested and popular simple addresses covering the varied themes of the Christian church year.

Rev. E. Charles Bauer knows how to speak to children. He is skilled also in conveying the lesson of a text—no matter how abstract. By means of visual illustrations the point of the Scripture lesson is made vivid and memorable, and leaders who use these talks will find the illustrations readily available or adaptable to their own setting and needs.

These 56 talks will supply the leader with a meditation for every Sunday and festival of the church year, plus a few extra. Simple, straightforward prayers can be composed for the "congregation" —or by them—on the basis of the text and exposition. Within the seasons, the talks can be transposed to suit the local theme of the day—or they may provide the theme of the worship as they are delivered in succession.

The author's consistent accent on the child's relationship to God in Christ provides motivation and power for the life in Christ to which the hearer is led.

Behold, the days are coming, says the Lord, when I will fulfill the promise I made to the house of Israel and the house of Judah. (Jeremiah 33:14)

Lost and Found

If you get lost in the woods, a compass will help you to find your way because compasses tell you where north and south, east and west are. But compasses do not tell us where people are. If a little boy gets lost in a big department store, a compass will not tell him where his mother is. Only a policeman or someone who really knows his way around can help the little fellow get back to his mother.

Now, of course, you know that *all* the children of Adam and Eve, all of God's children, all of us, the whole human race, got lost. We did not get lost in the woods; we did not just lose our mother in the store, but we lost our heavenly Father, our best Friend. When Adam and Eve sinned, they got lost, and everyone else got lost with them. Just a compass would not be enough to help us find our heavenly Father again. He knew that we could never find Him without the help of someone who really knows his way around.

When a policeman finds a lost little boy or girl, we say the policeman *saves* the child. He is the child's savior. Well, God knew that His children needed a Savior too. And because He loves them so much, God promised His children that He would send them a

Savior, who would help them find Him and show them the way to heaven. You know whom He was going to send to save us—His own Son, Jesus. And you know that Jesus did come on Christmas Day so we could find God and not be lost anymore.

Wouldn't it have been terrible if God had not promised us a Savior, if we could never find God again, if we had to stay lost forever? If Jesus never came, we would have no hope of being saved, of getting to heaven—it would be just hopeless.

But now we can say: "To Thee, O Lord, I lift up my soul. O my God, in Thee I trust" (Ps. 25:1). That is what we should be doing during Advent, from now until Christmas—lifting our souls up to God and trusting in Him, remembering that Jesus was promised as Savior to the lost human race. We should be saying: "Let none that wait for Thee be put to shame" (Ps. 25:3). During Advent we should be looking for Jesus, not for Santa Claus; we should be standing up straight and raising our heads because our redemption is near, not because tinsel and ribbon and mistletoe are near. Advent is the time when we say: "Show us Thy steadfast love, O Lord, and grant us Thy salvation" (Ps. 85:7), because we are lost and need someone to save us. Jesus will save us, He will find our Father for us, He will take us to heaven—if we are ready. Advent is the time to get ready.

Reading: Psalm 85:6-7

Please renew our strength, and we, Your people, will praise You. Show us Your constant love, Lord, and give us Your saving help. (Psalm 85:6-7)

Gifts We Cannot See

My right hand is full of money. My left hand is full of life and happiness, of kindness and salvation. Which do you want: the money you can see in one hand or the things you cannot see in the other? Of course, you know a lot of people would grab the money, wouldn't they? And right now a lot of people are getting ready for Christmas—just with money. All they are thinking about are the presents that money can buy—the things that you can see and hear and feel, the things that are in the store window and that you can cart home and wrap up and hand out with beautiful bows on them.

But are those the only Christmas gifts? Is that all Christmas means? Are the only presents we are waiting for the ones with beautiful bows on them, the ones that cost money? Well, if that is all we are waiting for, then we are going to miss the boat—or the sleigh.

This money is nice, and I can do a lot of good things with it. The Christmas gifts with the beautiful bows on them are nice, too, and we all like to get them. The tinsel and trees, the ribbons and bells, the glitter and lights—all of those things are nice. But they are not the things that really count. The things that

16

money can buy, that we can see and hear and feel and taste are not the things that make Christmas. They are not the real Christmas presents.

The real Christmas presents are life and happiness, kindness and salvation: the life of God, the happiness of heaven, the kindness of Jesus, the salvation of souls. Those are the gifts that we cannot see or hear, feel or taste, the gifts which really make Christmas because the Son of God came from heaven on that day to bring them to us. They are not things of earth, but things of heaven, the things we pray today that God will help us to *want,* the things we should be getting ready for and waiting for during Advent. Let's really *mean* the prayer: "Please renew our strength, and we, Your people, will praise You. Show us Your constant love, Lord, and give us Your saving help."

Reading: Isaiah 61:1-11

I will greatly rejoice in the Lord, my soul shall exult in my God. (Isaiah 61:10)

What Christmas Joy Really Is

"I can hardly wait!" That is what we say when we know something nice is going to happen. (Ring of alarm clock) But not when we have to get up in the morning. When we are going to have company, when there is going to be a party, when we are going to get a present, we can hardly wait.

That is the way God's people were feeling about the Savior. They knew someone was coming to save them. They knew that God had promised to send someone to free His people from sin and hell and the devil. And they were getting excited. They wondered if John the Baptist was the Savior. They could hardly wait to find out, so they asked him: "Are you the One?" And they kept at him: "Who are you, who are you?" And of course, when John told them that he was not the Savior, many people must have been sad and disappointed because they could hardly wait.

We are lucky because we know that Jesus is the Savior, and we know that He came on Christmas to save us. And that is why we can hardly wait for Christmas to come again. It is only a couple of weeks away now, and so our prayers today are full of happiness. We can hardly wait for Christmas to get here so we can celebrate the coming of Christ. So we start celebrating today: "We rejoice with holy exultation," we say. "With holy exultation" does not mean that we are celebrating with food and drink and presents and decorations. It means we are full of happiness *inside* — in our hearts and souls. It is a *holy* happiness that fills our hearts because we can hardly wait for *Christ* to come.

The thing that makes us happy is that Christmas is coming again, and Christmas is Christ's birthday.

We are happy that He was born because He was born to save us, to free us from sin and hell and the devil. We are happy because God kept His promise and sent us a Savior. *That* is why St. Paul keeps telling us to be happy, to rejoice. Remember what he says: "Rejoice *in the Lord* always." And remember what we sing in our Advent song: "Rejoice! Rejoice, O Israel!" Why? Because "to you shall come Emmanuel." That's what "holy exultation" is: being happy that Christmas is coming *because* it is the *Lord's birthday.* So "rejoice *in the Lord!*"

Reading: Matthew 1:18-24

Behold, a virgin shall conceive and bear a Son, and His name shall be called Emmanuel (which means, God with us). (Matthew 1:23)

Christ Is Coming

Do you believe in Santa Claus? Some people do and some people don't. *Is* there a Santa Claus? For some people, yes; for some people, no. If you do *not* believe in Santa Claus, there *isn't* any—for *you.* But if you *do* believe in him, then there *is* a Santa Claus.

As far as Christmas goes, it really doesn't make much difference if there is a Santa Claus or not, because Christmas is not *his* birthday.

Christmas is the birthday of Christ. That is why we call it Christ-mas, or Christmas, because Jesus Christ was born on that day. So it makes a lot of difference whether you believe in *Him* or not. If you do not believe in Santa Claus, there can still be a Christmas; but if you do not believe in Christ, that is the end of Christmas. If Jesus was not born, then He does not have a birthday. If the Son of God did not come down on earth, then there is no reason to be happy at Christmas, no reason to celebrate, no reason for stars and carols, wreaths and trees, bells and angels, ribbons and bows.

But there *is* reason to celebrate, there is reason to be happy, there is reason to rejoice with holy exultation. Why? Because we have faith in God's promises. And we believe that God promised Christ our Lord and Savior. That is the only reason for us to be happy, the only reason for us to celebrate, the only reason for us to *have* Christmas at all—because we believe that Christ was born on that day.

We say it whenever we say, "I believe in one Lord, Jesus Christ . . . who for us men and for our salvation came down from heaven . . . and was made man." We *say* we believe in Christ, we believe He was born, we believe Christmas is His birthday. Then let's *act* that way. Believing isn't just saying so. Believing is *doing*. Doing what Christ wants means believing in Him. Believing in Him means God kept His promise.

If God kept His promise, then the Savior came. And if the Savior came — well, that doesn't mean that there really is a Santa Claus. But if the Savior came, then it does mean that there really is a Christmas.

Reading: Acts 13:16-25

It was Jesus, one of the descendants of David, that God made the Savior of the people of Israel, as He had promised. (Acts 13:23)

Jesus Was Born to Save Us

This is an Advent wreath. It has four candles, and we light one for each week of Advent. So when we come to Christmas Eve, we have all four candles lighted. With the four candles burning, what does it make you think of? Yes, it looks something like a birthday cake too. All during Advent we have been getting ready for the birthday of Jesus. And now the day before His birthday we have the whole wreath lighted because we can hardly wait.

That is the whole idea of Christmas Eve. We have been getting ready for Christmas all during Advent, and now we just can't wait any longer. Christmas Eve is something like lighting up the birthday cake a day ahead of time. Why? Why do we want so much for Christmas to come? Why can we hardly wait for our Lord's birthday?

Well, did you ever notice how many boys and girls tell you, "My birthday is next Tuesday," "I'm having company next Sunday," "I'm going home next week"? You see, whenever something wonderful is going to happen, it makes us happy. We always want important things to hurry up and happen.

Now, you know that the most wonderful, the most important thing of all happened on Christmas. It is Jesus who was born. And He was born to save us. That's why we tell each other in church today: "This day you shall know that the Lord will come and *save* us. And in the morning you will see the glory of the Lord" (Ex. 16:7). "Tomorrow shall the wickedness of the earth be wiped away." "The *Savior* of the world shall rule over us." "All mankind shall see the *salvation* of our God." "And you are to name Him Jesus, because He will *save* His people from their sins." (Matt. 1:21)

Tomorrow is the day Jesus was born. He was born to save us from our sins. That's the most wonderful thing that ever happened to us. That is what happened to us on His birthday. No wonder we want His birthday to hurry up and happen!

Reading: Psalm 97

Light shines on the righteous, and gladness on the good. (Psalm 97:11)

The Light of the World

Darkness can be a terrible thing. In darkness we cannot see what things look like. In darkness we cannot find our way. In darkness it does not matter what we do or how we dress or how we look, for we cannot be seen. In darkness almost nothing can grow. In darkness very few things can live. Darkness means not seeing. Darkness means not knowing. Darkness means not living. Darkness is death.

But "a light shall shine upon us this day; for the Lord is born to us." "He [is] the real Light that gives light to every man." "Today a Savior has been born to you." "And this life [is] the light of men. The Light shines on in the darkness." "All the ends of the earth have seen the salvation of our God."

No wonder there are lights and stars, tinsel and glitter all over the world today. No wonder that we try to find every bright, shining, glowing thing there is to make Christmas sparkle and glimmer with as much light as we can. No wonder that the words "light" and "sight," "seeing" and "shining" are used so many times in our worship at Christmas. For "this day a great light has [come down] upon the earth." This day "a Child is born to us, a Son is given to us,"

23

and "we have been newly enlightened by the Word made flesh."

Now we can find our way. Now we can see what things look like. Now we can have life. The darkness of sin, the darkness of ignorance, the darkness of death is gone. "May our deeds reveal the light of faith that shines in our hearts." May we always do what we can now see is the right thing to do, so that "we who have known the mystery of Christ's light on earth may also enjoy His happiness in heaven." And even now, may all your Christmases be bright!

Reading: Galatians 4:1-7

So then, you are no longer a slave, but a son. And since you are His son, God will give you all He has for His sons. (Galatians 4:7)

You Are a Son!

In my hands I am holding a beautiful Christmas package. But see what happens when I open it: there is nothing inside. This package is very pretty, but if I gave it to you for Christmas, would you say it was the best gift you got? I should say not! You would say that it was just a fake: pretty on the outside, but nothing on the inside.

When you stop to think about it, most Christmas presents are like that. Delicious candies, cakes, and cookies are all gone after we eat them. Beautiful shirts and dresses are all worn out by next Christmas. The sweetest powder and perfume, the best cigars and cigarettes are all blown away, poured out, burnt to pieces, or gone up in smoke after a few days or weeks.

You see how beautiful something can be on the outside — like this package — and yet inside there is nothing. The best Christmas gift of all is not something that "looks" beautiful. It is something *inside,* which we cannot see, but where it really counts. St. Paul tells us today in four words what the best gift of all is: "You are a son!" And he says: "The proof that you are sons is the fact that God has sent forth *into our hearts* the Spirit of *His Son* who cries out, 'Abba' ('Father')."

What a Christmas gift! God sent His Son to us on Christmas so we could be His children. Because Jesus came to save us, now we can call God "Father." The first people had turned away from God by sin. That turned all of God's people away from Him. Then on the first Christmas God's Son became one of God's people so that they could all turn back to God and be His sons again.

That is the best Christmas gift of all. It is not in a beautiful box. It is deep in our hearts, "the Spirit of His Son," by whom we dare to say: "Our Father who art in heaven." May we never forget to say: "Hallowed be Thy name"!

Reading: Titus 2:11-15

For God has revealed His grace for the salvation of
all men. . . . He gave Himself for us, to rescue us from
all wickedness and make us a pure people who belong
to Him alone. (Titus 2:11, 14)

This Year Ask for Help
When You Need It

I am going to break this stick. You saw me break
it. Now what would you think if I said, "*It* broke"?
If I let the stick lay here, it would never, never break
itself. *I* did it. I cannot say, "*It* broke," but I have to
say, "*I* broke *it*."

Sometimes people try to "get out of things" by
blaming "things" for what happens. It's always the
same old tune, "*It* broke." When people say that, they
are saying, "*I* didn't break it; it is not *my* fault; *I* can't
help it." Have you been singing that tune over and
over again? Have you been saying time after time,
"I can't help it if I swear; I can't help it if I disobey;
I can't help it if I get mad; I can't help it if I answer
back, lie, steal, miss my prayers"? If you have been
singing that same old tune over and over, then it is
time to "sing to the Lord a new song."

And this is the perfect time to start singing a new
song at the beginning of a New Year. If you have been
saying you can't *help* it when you do wrong, then make
up your mind you are going to *get* the help you need
not to do wrong. Remember that "God has revealed

26

His grace for the salvation of *all* men." Remember that "He gave Himself for us, to rescue us from all wickedness."

There is the whole idea of Christmas: Jesus came to *help* us to be good. Right now on this New Year's Day let's make up our mind that we are not going to sing the same old tune this year, "I can't help it." *This* year let's "sing to the Lord a *new* song." When we *need* help, let's *ask* for it. Say it over and over: "Lord, help me!" Then you will have a happy new year! I hope you do!

Reading: Isaiah 60:1-7

Your light has come, the glory of the Lord shines upon you. (Isaiah 60:1)

Keep the Light of Grace Shining

Most people do not like the dark. And nobody wants to be in the dark all the time. (Lights out.) This is not so bad, because there is still some light in here. But if it were pitch dark, as black as a coal mine, you would not want to stay here very long.

And that's the way it was in the world for thousands of years. When the first people sinned, they turned off the light of God's grace. The darkness of sin filled the soul of every man, woman, and child. It was so dark in the souls of men that no one would ever be able to see God—unless somehow the light of grace could be turned on.

Well, when the darkness of sin started—way back at the beginning—God promised that He would send a Savior who would bring the light of grace, the light of salvation to the world. And that is what happened on the first Christmas: the Savior was born, and in a little dark cave the light of grace began to shine. (Lights on in manger.)

At first only Mary and Joseph and a few Jewish shepherds saw Jesus. The Savior was a Jewish baby, and for a while only the Jewish people could see the light of salvation. But then a star began to shine. Several wise men from far, far away saw the star and knew that it was a very special one. They followed the star until it brought them to the Savior. For the first time people who were *not* Jewish saw the light of salvation. (Sanctuary lights on.) When the Wise Men came to Bethlehem, it meant that Jesus had come, not just to save the Jewish people. It meant that the Christ Child was the Savior of the world.

Today is Three Kings' Day or the Feast of the Epiphany. It is the day when we remember that the light of grace started to shine for all the people of the world. (Nave lights on.) What a difference that made for all of God's people. Now the darkness of sin could be put out of everyone's soul. Now everyone could someday be saved, could see God's love.

How lucky we are! The light of grace started shining in our hearts the minute we were baptized. And it will keep on shining as long as we are God's children. And someday we will really see God in heaven.

Every time you see a star — in the sky or anywhere else — remember how lucky you are to have the light of grace. Every time you see a star, be sure to tell your Savior that you are going to keep that light shining in your heart by loving Him and living for Him.

Reading: Luke 2:41-52

He answered them, "Why did you have to look for Me? Didn't you know that I had to be in My Father's house?" (Luke 2:49)

Heaven, Our Real Home

The first thing someone said to me this morning was "Welcome home." I was away last week, and it was nice to have someone welcome me back — not just to "my house" but to my *home*. Did you ever stop to think about the difference between a house and a home?

Maybe you go to the dentist in a regular, ordinary-looking house where other dentists or doctors have their offices. But does anyone ever call that house a home? Right next door might be a great big brick building, an apartment house. It is not really a house, but it *is* a home. Why? Well, the first place was only a house because nobody lived there; and the great big building is a home because people live in it. I was welcomed home this morning, because this is where I *live*. And that is exactly what makes a home: a place where there is life, because people live in it.

The little house at Nazareth was a home because a family lived in it. And it was a very holy home because the *Holy* Family lived there, Jesus, Mary, and Joseph. There was good life in that house, so it was a good home.

Now, where do you suppose the best home of all is? Well, I guess everybody knows that; heaven is the best home of all, because the best kind of life is there. We call it "eternal life." Eternal life means life that will never, never end, everlasting life. But it means more than that. It means the happiest and holiest kind of life, because it is God's life. God has eternal life, and we call heaven His eternal home, because it is where He lives.

But heaven is *our* eternal home, too, because we can live there with God someday, because we can have that happy, holy life which never ends. In fact, that is the whole idea; it is the only reason we are here, the only reason God made us, so we can live with Him forever, and that is why heaven is our real, true home.

Dear God, it will be wonderful "to be welcomed by You into Your eternal home." It will be wonderful if You are glad to see us. It will be wonderful to live the best life of all in our real home. I want to live with You forever and ever. Amen.

Reading: Psalm 148

Praise Him, all His angels, all His heavenly armies! (Psalm 148:2)

When Jesus Showed His Glory

Do you remember when we looked at the three people in Jesus' family? Today I would like you to take three looks at one of those people, Jesus. In the first look you see the baby Jesus, in the second, the boy Jesus, and in the third, the man Jesus. (Show 3 pictures) That is exactly what the church has been showing us for the last three weeks: on Christmas and New Year's we saw our Lord as a little baby in the crib, last Sunday we saw Jesus as the boy at Nazareth, and today He is the man at the wedding feast.

But is Jesus only a little baby, only a young boy, only a grown man? At Bethlehem and at Nazareth He may look like any other baby or any other boy. But at Cana today is He just like every other man at that wedding party? You know what happened at the party: they ran out of wine, and nobody could do a thing about it—except Jesus. No other man at that wedding feast could change water into wine—except Jesus. Not a single other person there could do such a thing—except Jesus—because changing water into wine is a miracle, and only God can do miracles. But Jesus did that miracle, He changed water into wine, He did what no other man at Cana could do to show that He is not like any other man. He did what only God can do to show that He is not *just* a man, but that He is God too. As the Gospel story says, "He revealed His glory." Everybody could see that He was a baby at Bethlehem. Everybody could see that He was a boy at Nazareth. Everybody could see that He was a man at Cana. But besides that, at Cana we can all see that He is God too, because He does what only God can do.

That is why we "praise the Lord" today. That is why we say, "Let all on earth worship You—and sing praise to You." That is why we "sing praise to the glory of His name." Because Jesus is the name, not just of a little baby, not just of a good boy, not just of a great man. Jesus is our God. "Praise Him, all you hosts. Alleluia!"

If someone does evil to you, do not pay him back with evil. Try to do what all men consider to be good. (Romans 12:17)

Do Not Try to Get Even

When Jesus was dying on the cross, people going by laughed at Him, called Him names, and said all kinds of awful things to Him. And what did Jesus do? Did He curse those people and swear at them? Did He ask His Father to blind them or cripple them or strike them dead? No, Jesus said, "Father, forgive them; they do not know what they are doing." When people hurt our Lord, He never hurt them back, but was kind and good to them.

Is that the way we are? Are we kind and good to people when they hurt us? I guess not! When anyone does something we don't like, we try to "get even" or "get back" at him. But is that what we *should* do, what *God* wants us to do? God has said, "Vengeance belongs to Me; I will repay." Vengeance means "getting back" at someone or "getting even" with him. But God tells us that *He* is the one to take care of that, that *He* will punish people when they do wrong. It is not up to *us* to do it. St. Paul says, "Do not avenge yourselves." He means the same thing that God says: Don't try to get even with people.

So God and St. Paul both tell us that we should not be mean just because someone else is mean. And

Jesus *shows* us how to act: be kind and good to other people even when they are not kind and good to us.

Is that easy? No! We would rather "get even." But that is not the right thing to do. Jesus showed us the right thing: He *prayed* for those who were against Him. He will help *us* to *do* the right thing too—if we ask Him. From now on when someone says or does something you don't like, *ask* God to help you; then ask Him to help the one who hurt you. Instead of cursing, swearing, or "getting even," just say: "Jesus, help me—Jesus, help him—or her." That's the best way to "get even."

Reading: Psalm 118

The Lord's mighty power has done it! His power has brought us victory, His mighty power in battle! I will not die, but I will live and tell what the Lord has done. (Psalm 118:15-17)

God Is Our Strength

I guess everyone knows who Superman is. All of you have seen him, on television or in the movies, flying through the air. You have seen him climb walls and catch cannonballs. You have seen him lift ships out of the water and twist the wings off airplanes. Superman is supposed to be able to do anything. But, of course, you know that he can't really do anything, because all those powerful things you see him doing are just make-believe. They are camera tricks which make it look as though he can do a lot of things which he really cannot do.

In the Gospel picture of the apostles on a stormy lake you see someone doing something that no one else can do. There is a big storm on the sea. It is tossing a boat around like a matchstick, and the men in the boat are scared to death. They yell for help, and a Man who is sleeping in the boat gets up, speaks to the wind and the waves, and the storm stops. Could Superman do that? Could he make the winds and the sea do what he tells them? Never! But the Man in the boat could do it, because the Man is Jesus, and Jesus is God.

The other men in the boat, the apostles, could not stop the storm any more than a superman could. All they could do was holler for help: "Lord, save us!" That is the way all of us feel sometimes; we are so helpless by ourselves. When the storms of trouble and sickness and temptation come up, we are too weak to do anything about it.

It would have been silly for the apostles to start shouting at the storm. If they just kept telling the wind and the waves to go away, it wouldn't have done any good at all. But they were smart. They knew they were not strong enough to stop the storm, so they called on someone who could do something about it.

That is what we will do, too, if we are smart. In our prayers we tell God how weak we are and how much we need His help. Let's remember that every day: we are weak, but God is strong. When things are too hard or too big or too heavy for us, let us be smart and remember how many times "the Lord's mighty power has done it." When we need help, let us be sure to ask for it. There isn't any Superman to help us, but there is a God who will never let us down, no matter how big the storm is. All we have to say is, "Lord, save us!"

Reading: Colossians 3:12-17

Everything you do or say, then, should be done in the name of the Lord Jesus, as you give thanks through Him to God the Father. (Colossians 3:17)

Everything in the Name of Jesus

This is a ten-dollar bill. It is no good to you. It is mine. You cannot do anything with it so long as it is mine. But see what happens when I put the bill in this envelope which has your name on it. Now the ten dollars is for you and can do you some good—because I am giving it to you. If I keep the money, it will help me, but if I give it to you, it will help you. The ten-dollar bill is worth something to *me* if I keep it. It is worth something to *you* if I give it away.

But do you know that some things are worth a lot more to us if we give them away? In fact *every*thing can be worth more if we give it—to God. That is what St. Paul means when he says: "Everything you do or say . . . should be done in the name of the Lord Jesus." It is the reason, too, why we say in the morning prayer: "Father in heaven, I give to you today, all I think and do and say." That is just like putting God's name on everything you think and do and say all day long.

Now let's suppose that you have to mop the floor. You grumble and gripe and groan about it. You curse Mrs. What's-her-name because she told you to do it. You are ugly all the rest of the day because you had to do a little work. Does the mopping do you any good? Not a bit! But suppose you give it away! Suppose you do the mopping for God. Suppose you sing and smile and are happy because you have a chance to do what *God* wants. Suppose you say, "It's not just Mrs. What's-her-name who wants me to do it! It's God who wants it. I am going to put *His* name on it. I am going to give it to Him—then it will be worth something."

No matter what it is—working, sleeping, praying, eating, drinking, playing—everything will do us a lot more good if we do it for God. This ten-dollar bill is worth ten dollars to me if I *keep* it. Everything else is worth a lot more if I *give* it — to God. I hope you will be sure to say that morning prayer every single day — then you will be putting God's name on everything you think and do and say.

Reading: Matthew 20:1-16

You also go to work in the vineyard, and I will pay you a fair wage. (Matthew 20:4)

God Is Fair

Every cow knows that the grass is always greener on the other side of the fence. Did you ever see a great big cow or a little lamb with her head stuck through a fence, eating the grass on the other side? There is always lots of beautiful green grass right under the poor animal's feet, but she practically chokes herself on the fence to get what is on the other side.

Well, I guess you can't blame a poor little lamb or a great big cow, but the trouble is that *people* do the same thing. Cows and lambs don't know any better, but men and women and boys and girls are supposed to know that the grass is *not* greener on the other side of the fence. How about you? Do you ever think it is?

Oh, *yes,* you do! How many times I hear people complain about this and that and the other thing! How many times you say, "He gets this," or, "She gets that, and what do I get?" How many times you think that God does not listen to your prayers. How many times you say, "It ain't fair!"

And that is exactly what the fellows said in today's Gospel story. They said the employer was not fair because he paid some workers more than others. They thought the other fellow's grass was greener. But the employer was not unfair. Each one got just what he was supposed to get. The trouble was that they were all looking over the fence at the other fellow, instead of minding their own business.

And that's the trouble with us too. God does not give us all the same things, but He does give each one of us what we need and whatever is best for us —just as He gives every cow and lamb the grass it needs right on its own side of the fence. We can be sure that God is never unfair, even if people are. He will always pay us what is fair. And if we look over the fence at the other fellow and complain, then God can say, "My friend, I am doing you no injustice. Take your pay and go home. I choose to give this man who was hired last the same pay as you, and I said, 'I'll pay you whatever is fair.'"

I am ashamed to admit it: we were too timid to do that! . . . If I must boast, I will boast of things that show how weak I am. (2 Corinthians 11:21, 30)

I Will Boast About My Weaknesses

I am sure you won't be able to see it because it is so tiny, but I have here a little flower seed. I hope it will grow. Then you will be able to see it. Oh! I have to *plant* it if I want it to grow. Well, I just happen to have a nice, clean flower pot with me. There! Dirt and water? Just a moment. That's right! All it took was a little dirt and water, and look at that—a beautiful plant.

Well, I guess you know that seeds do not work that way. They never grow in a minute. They have to be planted in good ground; they have to have water and sunshine; you have to dig around them and weed them; you have to give them time. *Then* after a lot of time and work, after a lot of sun and rain, someday the seeds will grow into beautiful, big plants.

You see, seeds are pretty small and weak. By themselves they can never amount to much. But when they have the help they need to grow, those weak, little seeds can give us flowers, fruits, vegetables, and even trees. We have lumber and food and beauty because weak, little seeds can grow into big, strong plants.

In that long, long passage we have just read St. Paul tells us how weak he is. He tells us all his troubles. He tells us that he's not strong enough to do very much and that he feels quite little. But, he says, because I am so weak and small, God will help me. Then I will really be able to get somewhere. Like the little, weak seed, I will really be able to become something different — *if* I have the help I need.

Now, how about us? Sometimes it seems that we are never going to get anywhere, that we are never going to make anything out of ourselves. It is so hard to be good, to fight sin, to win the war with the devil. We are so small and weak! How can we do it?

That's what St. Paul said. But *God* said: "I am big and strong. I will help you." And that's what He will say to us, too, if we will just be honest enough to say that we are small and weak. If we are honest enough to say we cannot make anything out of ourselves — just like the tiny seed — then *God* will make something out of us. St. Paul wasn't afraid to say that he needed help. Don't be afraid to say that you need help, either. God knows that we are weak and small. If *we* know it, too, He will be able to help us.

Reading: Luke 18:35-43

"What do you want Me to do for you?" "Sir," he answered, "I want to see again." (Luke 18:41)

Put God First

Please cover your eyes with your hand. Now, keep them covered tight—no fair peeking. All covered? All right. Now, tell me what I have in my hand. You can't tell me, can you?—because you cannot see. Now, everybody, uncover your eyes. Now you see what I have: a beautiful flower.

Do you know that some poor people's eyes are closed all the time like the man's in today's Gospel story? They are blind. They never see anything. Isn't that terrible, not to be able to see anything? Wouldn't it be terrible if *you* were blind? You could never see this beautiful flower—or any flower. You could never see the bright sun or the pretty sky. You would never know what anyone looks like. You could not see what you are eating or where you are going or what you are doing. That would be awful, wouldn't it?

But there are other things that we "see" with our hearts. We can "see" that people are good to us or love us. We "see" who our friends are—not with our eyes, but with our hearts. If your heart isn't blind, you can "see" who your best friend is—who loves you most of all, who is better to you than anyone else. You "see" that it is God.

Some people cannot see that, because their hearts

are blind. All they see is what they want to see. If you put your hand in front of your eyes, you cannot see me. All you can see is your hand. If you keep your hand there, it's almost like being blind, because your hand is in the way and you cannot see anything else.

That is what some people do with their hearts. They put something in the way so they cannot see how good God is. What is it they put in the way? Themselves! If you just look at yourself, if you just think of yourself, if you just love yourself, will you see anyone else or think of anyone else or love anyone else? No!—just yourself! That means that you will not love God or think of Him or see how good He is, either. If we want to see how beautiful God is, we have to get ourselves out of the way, just as you have to get your hand away from your eyes if you want to see this beautiful rose.

During Lent we are going to try to get ourselves out of the way so we can "see" God. The whole idea of Lent is to put God first, *before* ourselves—then we'll be able to "see" what He is like. I hope you will all ask God to help *you* to "see." He will—just like the blind man He helped long ago.

Reading: Psalm 91

When they call to Me, I will answer them; when they are in trouble, I will be with them. I will rescue them and honor them. I will reward them with long life, and will surely save them. (Psalm 91:15-16)

Satan's Sales Talk

You may have either one of these, this nice, juicy apple, or this little cross. Which one do you want? When I say that, I am giving you your choice, I am letting you take your pick. But now suppose I say: "Look at this beautiful apple. It is delicious, nice and ripe and juicy. Oh, will it ever taste good! You don't want this old cross, do you? You can't eat it. The cross won't do you any good. Why don't you take the apple? See how good it is. You may have the cross if you want it, but if I were you, I would take the apple. Go on — take the apple."

That's what we call a temptation. In the first place I just gave you your choice — you could choose either one. But then I really tried to get you to take the apple. You still could take your pick, but it would be pretty hard to choose the cross after I gave you such a "sales talk" about the apple.

And that's just about what a temptation is, a "sales talk" by the devil, telling us how much fun it will be to do something that God does not want us to do. You saw the devil giving a "sales talk" like that to Jesus Himself when he tempted Jesus. Three times he said, "Look how nice it will be if you do this or that or the other thing. Come on—turn against your heavenly Father; it will be so much fun!" The first people of God were given a "sales talk" like that too. They were tempted by the devil—and they gave in; they gave in to the devil and let him "sell" them something that God did not want them to do. Jesus did not give in, He did not "buy" what the devil was trying to sell, He chose the *right* thing.

Do you think the devil has stopped tempting God's people? You can stay home or come to church, you can lie or tell the truth, you can steal or be honest, you can disobey or mind, you can curse or pray. Does the devil just say, "Take your pick?" You bet he doesn't! He gives you a big "sales talk" about how much fun it will be to stay home, lie, steal, disobey, curse. He tempts you to take the apple and throw away the cross. What are you going to do: take the apple, like the first people of God, or take the cross, like the Son of God?

Jesus showed us how to do the right thing: by "calling upon God." God tells everyone who is tempted how to do the right thing too: "When they call to Me, I will answer them."

This is God's will for you: He wants you to be holy . . . .
God did not call us to live in immorality, but in holiness. (1 Thessalonians 4:3, 7)

How to Stay Good

I wonder how many of you ever saw a movie
called *Dr. Jekyll and Mr. Hyde.* If you did, you probably remember that Dr. Jekyll and Mr. Hyde were
not two different people — they were both the same
fellow: a fellow who was sometimes very nice and
kind and helpful — that's when he was Mr. Hyde; but
then the same fellow would change into a terrible
monster who would steal and burn and kill — that's
when he was Dr. Jekyll.

Now, do you remember what happened to Jesus
in the desert when He was tempted by the devil?
He went without food and drink for 40 days, and
He was hungry. That showed that He was human
like us. But look at Jesus when He is transfigured
on the mountain: His face is as bright as the sun, and
His clothes shine like light. That shows that Jesus
is divine. So our Lord is a man, but not just an ordinary man, because He is God too. He is not two different people; He is just one Person, the Son of God,
the Second Person of the Holy Trinity, but He is God
and man at the same time.

Of course you know that Jesus is not like Dr.
Jekyll and Mr. Hyde. He is not God one day and

man the next. But sometimes *we* are Dr. Jekylls and Mr. Hydes, aren't we? Right now everybody here is like Mr. Hyde, nice and quiet, listening and praying and behaving himself. But how were you yesterday, and how will you be tomorrow? — a Dr. Jekyll, screaming, quarreling, fighting, cursing, swearing, disobeying? Nobody knew that the nice Mr. Hyde was really the awful Dr. Jekyll. Maybe you were so bad yesterday that people don't know you are the same boy or girl today.

When we look at Jesus loving us and suffering for us, it helps us to get the badness out of ourselves. It helps us be more like the nice Mr. Hyde and stop being like the awful Dr. Jekyll. It helps us to be less like a poor, weak man and more like God. And that is why the Son of God came to be like *us* — so He could help *us* be like *Him*. He became a man, so we could be like God.

When we remember Jesus and His cross, when we say our prayers, confess our sins, and listen to His Word — these things all help us to be more like God, they help us to stop being a Dr. Jekyll and Mr. Hyde by making us *stay* good — the way we are right now.

I look to the Lord for help at all times, and He rescues me from danger. (Psalm 25:15)

Leave It Up to the Lord

Anyone who sees this shamrock today will surely not think of Chief Sitting Bull or of the Queen of Sheba. No, today everybody is Irish and the shamrock means St. Patrick to everyone. They say he taught the Irish people about the Holy Trinity with the shamrock: three leaves in one plant — three Persons in one God. They also say there is not a single snake in Ireland today, because St. Patrick drove them all out.

Well I don't know if he got rid of all the snakes for the Irish, but if he did, it's no wonder they like St. Patrick, because hardly anybody likes snakes. But I do know that Jesus got rid of the devil, and He will get rid of him for everyone — not just for the Irish.

Do you remember the time in the desert when our Lord sent the devil away from Himself? And He sent the devil away from others too. God doesn't want anything to do with the devil — and He doesn't want His people to have anything to do with him, either.

There may not be any snakes in Ireland, but the devil is still around — everywhere. We saw him tempting Jesus, and we all know that He tempts us. He tries and tries to get us to do wrong, to turn against God, to follow him.

God wants us to change things around—to turn against the devil and follow God. We do that when we love God, when we are sorry for our sins, and when we do what God wants us to do. We do it by "paying more attention" to God.

Remember, it was Jesus who sent the devil away from Himself; it was Jesus who sent the devil out of the dumb man; and it is Jesus who will send the devil away from us. We have to do our part, yes. But it is really our Lord who gets rid of the devil for us. Lent should help us to remember that and to say more and more: "I look to the *Lord* for help at all times, and *He* rescues me from danger." Maybe Patrick freed Ireland of snakes, but it's God Himself who frees us from the devil.

Reading: Psalm 125

As the mountains surround Jerusalem, so the Lord surrounds His people. (Psalm 125:2)

Say Yes to God

If you want to keep dogs and cats out of your yard, you put a fence around it. If you want to keep wild animals out of your camp, you build a fort around it. Many cities have stone walls around them to keep people out, and some places are kept safe by high mountains all around.

It takes a lot of boards or a lot of stones or a lot of mountains to go around a yard or a camp or a city to make it safe. But the Lord can be all around His people keeping them safe, like a row of mountains or a great wall, because He is God.

Our Lord takes care of His people. We see Jesus feeding a great big crowd of people with just five little loaves of bread and two little fishes. That was something only God could do — a miracle — and Jesus did it because He loves His people and does not want them to be hungry.

God's Word shows how Christ made us free by making us safe against sin and the devil. Over and over we are told that God makes us happy: Jesus feeds our souls, He is good to us, He gives us grace, He makes us feel better, He makes us strong.

No wonder we say that "the Lord surrounds His people"! How much God takes care of us! He is always saying yes to us. And the closer we get to Easter, the more we are going to see our Lord saying yes, until He finally says yes to the cross and dies on it for us.

In one of our prayers we say, "I rejoiced because they said to me, 'We will go up to the house of the Lord.'" We should be happy to go to God's house, happy to pray, happy to hear our Father, happy to say yes to our Lord, because He is always saying yes to us.

Think of how much God has done for us; think of how good He is to us; remember that "the Lord surrounds His people," taking care of us and keeping us safe, and you will keep on saying yes to Him as you think how good He has been to you.

Reading: John 10:31-39

Who do you think you are? (John 8:53)

Who Do You Pretend to Be?

Everyone here can see this bunch of grapes, but nobody would know that someone gave them to me for Christmas. Christmas? Yes—three months ago! *Now,* these are not real grapes. They are make-believe, artificial. Yes, these are not grapes at all. They are a fake!

Would you believe that that is what they called our Lord? After all the miracles He had performed, after all the good He had done, after all the wonderful things He had told them, they said, "Who do you think you are?" They were saying, "You must be kidding; you can't be God; you're a fake!"

That hurts! It always hurts to be called names.

But to be called a fake hurts more than anything else, because a fake is a liar. When an honest man is called a liar, it really hurts.

Jesus is not only an honest man; He is God. How can God be a liar, how can God be a fake? How it must have hurt when His own people thought that, when they said it, when they even wanted to stone Him to death for it! It must have hurt Him even more than the stones would have. And that's how it all started. The sufferings of Jesus all started because people would not believe Him, because they were against Him, because they thought He was a fake. And they ended by beating Him, crowning Him with thorns, and nailing Him to a cross—all because they thought He was a fake.

That's the way it is now too. Oh, we would never say our Lord is a fake! But aren't we against Him when we sin? When we do not do what He wants, aren't we saying "Who do you think you are" to God? When we do not listen to Him, aren't we saying, "You must be kidding"?

Especially during the Lenten season we think about the Passion of our Lord. "Passion" means "suffering." We should remember who made Jesus suffer: the people who said "Who do you think you are" long ago, *and* the people who act that way now—you and I.

Reading: Mark 16:1-8

Who will roll away the stone from the entrance to the grave for us? (Mark 16:3)

Nothing Can Keep Us from Jesus

Stones are heavy. The bigger they are, the heavier they are. This is just a little pebble. Anyone can lift it. We can all lift this one too – or even this one. But just imagine a stone big enough to fill up a whole doorway. We could never budge it. How in the world do you suppose those three little ladies thought they were going to move the stone that closed the doorway to the grave of Jesus?

They knew they couldn't do it. They even said, "Who will roll away the stone for us?" They knew they couldn't get into the grave with the big stone in the doorway. But they went to our Lord's grave anyhow. They went because they loved Jesus. They were going to get into that cave to take care of His body. And they weren't going to let any stone stop them – no matter how big it was. They just knew that the stone would get moved somehow or other – because they really wanted to get to Jesus.

Of course, you know what happened: when they got there, the grave was open and Jesus was gone. Our Lord had come back to life. Nobody else could do that by himself. And nobody else could move that stone by himself, either. But Jesus could do it because

He is God. He could bring Himself back to life, and He could roll the stone away. And He did it. He rolled the stone away, not just for those three women, but for all of His people. He came back to life for all of us — to show us that He can do anything and everything.

We might not have to move any stones to get to Jesus, but a lot of other things get in our way — mostly sin and the devil. But are we going to let those things stop us? That big stone did not stop the women on Easter morning — because they wanted to get to our Lord. Nothing can keep *us* from getting to Him, either, if we *want* to get to Him. He came back to life; He moved the stone. He will move anything that is in our way too — if we really want Him to.

Reading: John 20:24-31

These have been written that you may believe that Jesus is the Messiah, the Son of God, and that through this faith you may have life in His name. (John 20:31)

Baptism, the Life of Our Souls

Did you ever hear of "Sunday-go-to-meetin' clothes"? They were special clothes that people wore just on Sundays to go to church. All of you have your Sunday clothes on right now, but you do wear those good clothes on other days too—whenever you have to get "dressed up," whenever there is something "special."

Well, there was a day when certain people used to "take off" their special clothes. It was called the "Sunday for the changing of the white clothes." When the church first started, people were baptized on Easter. After they were baptized, they put on special white clothes and wore them for a whole week. So, if you were one of those people and were baptized on Easter, you would change from the special white clothes of Baptism to your regular clothes a week later.

Now, why did people wear those special white clothes when they were baptized? For the same reason that a girl wears her "party dress" to a party or you wear your Sunday clothes to church. Because Baptism is something special. Baptism is the best thing that ever happened to us because it made us God's friends. Those people thought that was such a wonderful thing that they wore special clothes for the whole week of their Baptism.

But why *white* clothes? When we are born, how is our soul? It is full of sin, isn't it? Original sin, the sin of Adam and Eve. When we are born, our soul does not have God's life in it. It is full of the death of sin. But when we are baptized, God puts His life into our soul and the sin is gone. White is the color of life. Even now when babies are baptized, they always wear white dresses to show that they are getting the life of God into their souls.

Maybe you don't have a white dress or a white suit, but you do have "Sunday clothes." Whenever you get dressed up for something special, try to think of your Baptism. When you put on your "Sunday best," think of the new life that God put into your soul when you were baptized. When you put on your good clothes, *thank* God for the heavenly life He gave you in Baptism. And whenever you put your best clothes away, promise God that you will always try to keep His life in your soul and never "put it away" by sinning.

Reading: John 10:11-16

I am the Good Shepherd. As the Father knows Me and I know the Father, in the same way I know My sheep and they know Me. (John 10:14-15)

Let the Good Shepherd Feed You

All of you remember what a shepherd is — a man who takes care of sheep. But *how* does he take care of them? He watches them, keeps them from getting hurt and getting killed, and sees that they don't get lost and that no one steals them. But is that *all* he does for the sheep? I wonder if you know what sheep and lambs eat? That's right — grass. Now suppose a shepherd took his sheep where there were only stones and rocks. They couldn't eat, could they? So the shepherd has to take his sheep where there is grass. He has to see to it that they can eat.

Jesus says He is the Good Shepherd. And, of course, you know that *we* are His sheep, because He takes care of us — our bodies and our souls. If He is the *Good* Shepherd, He must see to it that our souls have food. Grass is food for sheep. Bread and butter, meat and potatoes are food for our bodies. But what is the food of our souls? How does Jesus feed our souls?

With the best food of all — His *own* body and blood. Our Lord feeds our souls every time we go to Holy Communion. That is why we call the altar in church the Lord's table, because that's where you get the wonderful food for your soul. There Jesus feeds you with His very body and blood.

Holy Communion is what keeps our souls strong and healthy just as meat and potatoes keep our bodies strong and healthy. The more we go to Communion, the stronger we will be. Jesus is our Good Shepherd because He gives us this wonderful food. We will be good sheep if we eat it as much as we can.

Reading: John 16:16-22

Now you are sad, but I will see you again, and your hearts will be filled with gladness, the kind of gladness that no one can take away from you. (John 16:22)

Rough Road to Happiness

I saw a picture on a calendar, one time, of a great big dog scratching himself. Next to him was a little puppy looking at the big dog. The puppy's eyes were popping right out, and he was saying, "Be youse got fleas, too?" And the big dog answered him, "Sure I are – everybody do," and went right on scratching himself.

Now, that is not very good English, but in dog language it just means that all dogs have fleas; so no dog should be surprised when he itches. I am not sure that all dogs really do have fleas, but I do know that all people have troubles. And sometimes people are very surprised because they have troubles. Some people think that things should always go the way they want them to, that everything should be smooth and easy and they should be happy all the time.

Well, let me tell you: *that* is heaven. Being happy all the time and never having anything go wrong can happen only in heaven. And we are not in heaven. We are down on earth where everyone has troubles, where things go wrong, and where it is not always smooth and easy. God Himself told us it would be that way. Jesus said, "You will weep and go into mourning." He said, "You will grieve" and be "in pain." Remember that even our Lord had to suffer and die. St. Peter tells us that life is a battle. That's the way it is in this world: trouble for everybody.

Nobody can promise a dog that he won't have fleas. And nobody ever promised us that we would not have troubles. But Jesus did promise us that the troubles will be over with someday and that we will then be happy forever and ever: "I will see you again, and your hearts will be filled with gladness, the kind of gladness that no one can take away from you." Lots of things can take happiness away from us now, but nothing can take away the happiness of heaven when we get there.

Don't be surprised when things go wrong, when you have trouble and the road is rough. That's the road to heaven. Sometimes it's a very rough road. When it is, just remember how wonderful it will be at the end of the road. And keep praying: "O Lord, teach me to love the things of heaven."

Reading: John 16:5-14

But I tell you the truth: it is better for you that I go away. (John 16:7)

Look for the Silver Lining

"Two men looked out from prison bars: one saw mud, the other stars." Why did one see mud and one see stars? Simply because one was looking down and the other up. (Point arrow down and up) As long as you look down at the mud, that's what you will see—just plain mud, never stars. So it all depends on how you look at a thing. If you look the wrong way, everything will look dark and gloomy. If you want things to look bright and shining, then you will have to be sure you're looking at them in the right way. Only one side of a mirror is bright and shiny.

It is true that the world is full of trouble. Our lives are full of trouble too. But not everything is bad. There are a lot of good and wonderful and beautiful things in the world too. And there are a lot of nice things in our lives besides the things we do not like—just as there are stars *and* mud outside every prison window. And just as every prisoner can keep looking at the mud if he wants to, so you can look just at the troubles. But the smart prisoner will make himself feel a lot better by looking at the stars instead of the mud. So you and I will be much happier if we are smart enough to look at the good, the nice, the wonderful, the beautiful things instead of the troubles.

After church today I wish you would try to think of all the *good* things you can, all "the wondrous things the Lord has done." Think of "each good gift and every best favor [that] comes from above." Shout joyfully to God and say, "Hear now, while I declare what the Lord has done for me." If you are really honest, you will be surprised how many good things you have and how many nice people there are and what wonderful things happen to you and how filled the world is with beauty.

Then, after you think of all the good things, think of the apostles, whose hearts were "full of sorrow" because Jesus was going to leave them. Remember what our Lord said: "It is *better* for you that I go away." *They* thought it was bad. *He* knew it was good. Even the things that look bad to us are very often good for us. That is why they say every cloud has a silver lining. Even mud can be good—some people build houses out of it. It all depends on how you look at it. Let us pray that we will look at things the right way— that our "hearts may always be fixed upon *true* happiness."

Praise our God, all nations; let your praise be heard. He has kept us alive and has not allowed us to fall. (Psalm 66:8-9)

Praise to the Lord

"You are a good boy." "You are a pretty girl." "You did a good job." "I like your work." These are things we all like to hear because we all like a little praise now and then. We like to have people say nice things to us because it shows that they love us — and everybody wants to be loved.

God wants to be loved too. That is the big commandment: "You shall love the Lord your God with your whole heart and with your whole mind and with all your strength." We show that we love God by saying nice things to Him. And He likes to have us say those things because He wants us to praise Him. He said so in His very first law: "I am the Lord your God; you shall not have strange gods before Me" — or the way most of us learned it: "First, I must honor God."

Honor, praise, worship are words that mean saying nice things to God. The Bible is filled with words of honor and praise to God. Most of our church prayers are taken from the Bible, so it is no wonder that the liturgy is always filled with prayers like "Shout joyfully to God, all you on earth, sing praise to the glory of His name: proclaim His glorious praise." Worshiping is the most wonderful way of praising and honoring God. It is the very best way of saying nice things to God and of *doing* something nice for Him.

But why should we praise God? Why is it so important to show that we love Him? Well, the first reason is just because He is God, because He is our Father and we belong to Him. The second reason is because God *told* us to praise Him and *wants* us to praise Him. And then there are many other reasons which we find in the Bible and in the very words of every church service.

Listen to some of them: "Bless the Lord our God, you peoples, loudly sound His praise [because] He has given life to my soul and has not let my feet slip. Blessed be the Lord [because He] refused me not my prayer or His kindness." We praise God because "the Lord has delivered His people" — because He has saved us. We say that all good comes from Him and that He died to save us.

There are lots of reasons for us to love God. Remember to show your love for Him by saying nice things to Him. "Sing to the Lord, Alleluia; sing to the Lord; bless His name; announce His salvation day after day, Alleluia, Alleluia."

This Jesus, who was taken up from you into heaven, will come back in the same way that you saw Him go to heaven. (Acts 1:11)

Hope in the Lord

Have you ever been "down in the dumps"? Sure, everybody gets down in the dumps once in a while. It means that you feel bad, or "blue," as some people say. But have you ever *really* been down in the *dumps* — the place where people dump all their garbage and trash and junk? It's an awful place; it smells awful. I am sure no one who really goes down to the dumps wants to stay there.

Well, you know, if you really like junk and trash, rubbish and garbage, you can always find enough of it. You can stay down in the dumps if you want to. But who wants to? Anytime I have ever really gone to the dumps I wanted to get out of there as soon as I could. Nobody really wants to be unhappy and sad and gloomy. And God does not want us to be that way either.

We have been talking about all the good things that should make us happy. Even the black clouds have a silver lining, and many of the things that look bad are *really* good for us. So we should always hope for the best.

Oh, what a big word that is, "hope"! Hope is what keeps us out of the dumps. Hope is what makes us "look for the silver lining." Hope is what makes us say: "All you peoples, clap your hands, shout to God with cries of gladness," and, "God mounts His throne amid shouts of joy," and "Chant praise to the Lord, who rises on the heights of heaven." Hope is what made the angels say to the apostles: "Men of Galilee, why do you stand there looking up at the sky? This Jesus, who was taken up from you into heaven, will come back in the same way that you saw Him go to heaven."

That's what hope is: it makes us trust that God will make everything come out all right. The apostles were down in the dumps on that first Ascension Thursday when they saw Jesus taken away from them. But the angels gave them hope by promising that their Friend would come back again at the end of the world. Our Lord Himself had promised this over and over, but they missed the point. Let's make sure that *we* don't miss the point. Let's always remember that God will make things come out all right. Let's keep our chins up and stay out of the dumps by hoping in the Lord.

Reading: John 15:26—16:4

And the time will come when anyone who kills you will think that by doing this he is serving God. (John 16:2)

Forgive Everybody Who Hurts You

Once there was a Man who was good to everybody; He did everything He could to help people. He never hurt anyone. When they were hungry, He gave them things to eat; when they were sick, He made them well. He even told them how to be happy forever. He was their best friend. Some of those people got mad at Him, some ran away from Him, and finally some of them even killed Him.

Do you know who that Man was? Yes, it was Jesus. He was not only their best friend but their God. Did they have any reason to get mad at Him or run away from Him? Did they have any reason to *kill* Him? Is that what we should do to people who are nice to us, our friends?

Well, that is what they did to Jesus. Jesus tells us that people will do the same thing to us. He tells us that even when we are good to people, they will not always be good to us. Even when we are nice, people will not always be nice to us. Even when we help others, they will sometimes get mad at us.

Now, what did Jesus do when people treated Him that way? Did He get mad and curse and swear at them? Did He fight with them and call them names? I guess not! No matter what people did to Him, Jesus way always good to them. When they put Him on the cross, what did He do? He *prayed* for them. Even now, when *you* hurt Jesus by sin, what does He do? Does He hurt you? No! He helps you, He forgives you. He takes your sin away. He loves you.

Well, that is just the way Jesus wants us to be; He wants us to *forgive* people, no matter what they do to us. How do I know? Because that is just what He told us to say in the prayer He taught us: "Forgive us as we forgive those who sin against us."

It is easy to get mad and call names. It is not easy to forgive and be nice when people hurt us. But Jesus wants us to, and so He will help us to. He showed us how. He said, "Father, forgive them," when He was dying. He told us what to say: "Forgive us our trespasses as we forgive those who trespass against us." Jesus, help us to forgive; help us to be nice to people even when they are not nice to us. Help us to be like You!

Reading: Acts 2:1-11

Suddenly there was a noise from the sky which sounded like a strong wind blowing . . . . They were all filled with the Holy Spirit. (Acts 2:2,4)

Love in Action

This banner has something written on it, but you cannot read it because the word is hidden in the folds. It is something like a flag draped around a pole on a quiet day: you cannot see the stars and stripes very well. But when the wind starts to blow, what happens? The flag opens up and you can see every star and stripe. Something like this: when the fan starts to blow on the banner, it opens up, and then you can see what is inside the folds: LOVE.

On the first Pentecost the Holy Spirit came "like a strong wind blowing" and filled the hearts of the apostles with love. Did they just sit there, then, full of love? No sir! They got going. They went out and helped other people. They showed their love by *doing* something. The Holy Spirit did not just *fill* them with love. He got those men *moving*—just as this fan got the banner moving. That's what makes love mean something. This word did not mean a thing to you until we got the banner moving. It's the same way with us: the love in our hearts doesn't mean much until we get going and *do* something.

The Holy Spirit fills *our* hearts with love too. But He does more than that. He gets us going. He helps us to show our love by doing something for God and for God's people. When Jesus said we should love God above all things and our neighbor as ourselves, He did not mean that we should keep the love hidden in our hearts—like this word was hidden in the folds of the banner. He wanted us to *show* our love for Him by praying, coming to church, receiving Holy Communion, and being good. He wanted us to *show* our love for His people by helping others, being nice to them, and talking to them the way we should.

As we remember what happened on the first Pentecost, let's ask the Holy Spirit to *move* all of us—just as this fan is moving the banner—to *show* our love for God and for other people by doing something for them. Let us pray that all of us may be "filled with the Holy Spirit."

Reading: 2 Corinthians 13:11-13

The grace of the Lord Jesus Christ, the love of God, and the fellowship of the Holy Spirit be with you all. (2 Corinthians 13:13)

Three Persons—One God

I was a long way from here last week for a meeting in a place called Denver. On Monday, right in the middle of May, I drove through a big snowstorm. . . . Do you believe that? All right. Now here is a snowball which I brought back with me. Do you believe that? No? Well, you can see this, can't you? It *is* a snowball, isn't it? They say "seeing is believing," but it isn't, is it? Even though you can see this and it does look like a snowball, you know it is not, and you know I could not bring it back all the way from Denver even if it were a snowball. But it isn't, is it? But you do believe I drove through a snowstorm in Denver last Monday — even though you did *not* see the snowstorm. You believe it because I said so.

I believe you when you tell me something too. People are always believing one another. Well, if we can believe one another, we surely can believe God. When you tell me you have a toothache, I believe it — not because I *see* your toothache, but because I think you *know* when your tooth aches and because I think you *tell the truth.* Surely *God knows* what is true and *tells* the truth, because He knows everything and is all good — otherwise He could not be God. Someone who doesn't even know what he is talking about certainly cannot be in charge of everything.

We cannot *see* that there are three Persons in God, but we *believe* that there are three Persons in God *because* God said so. We have the Feast of the Holy Trinity — which means three Persons in one God. We have been baptized "in the name of the Father and of the Son and of the Holy Spirit" because Jesus told us to be. And we will bless God the Father, the Son, and the Holy Spirit "because He has shown His mercy to us."

71

We cannot *see* God's mercy; we cannot *see God* — and we cannot *see* that there are *three Persons* in God. That is something we believe because God said it, not because we have seen it. We confess this faith in the Creed, which we say every Sunday. Let us say it now — and mean it!

Reading: Luke 14:16-24

But they all began, one after another, to make excuses. (Luke 14:18)

Take the Blame if You Are Wrong

"Who? Me? Why I wouldn't do such a thing!" Did you ever say that when you were blamed for something? Or when you are being scolded, do you ever say, "Not *me!* He did it," or "Well, *she* started it," or "They *made* me do it"? And if you really get caught at something, do you always come up with "I couldn't *help* it?"

We never like to admit that we are wrong. But how do you think God likes it when we are always making excuses? How do you think that man felt after he had the big dinner ready and his friends made all kinds of excuses? The Bible tells us he was angry at them. He was mad because they really could have come to the banquet, but they just wanted to get out of it. Their poor excuses showed that they were not really very good friends of the man who invited them.

And our poor excuses show that we are not really very good friends of God, either. He does not like it when we make lame excuses. And because He is God, He knows when we are making poor excuses. He knows when something is really our fault.

As a matter of fact, we are not very good friends of anybody if we never take the blame, if everything is always the other fellow's fault. Nobody can be right *all* the time. All of us make mistakes sometimes. We all do wrong now and then. But if we blame everything that goes wrong on to somebody else, we will not have many friends, because everybody knows that we are to blame sometimes.

There is a good little prayer we can say: "O Lord, deliver me from lying lip." When I put the blame on somebody else, when I am wrong and point my finger at the other fellow, I am *lying,* and nobody loves a liar. If you have been bad, admit it. When you are wrong, take the blame. Ask the Lord to keep you from making lame excuses. Ask the Lord to keep you from lying. If you want to make strong friends, don't make weak excuses. If you are true to God, you cannot lie to men. "O Lord, deliver me from lying lip."

Reading: Luke 15:1-7

This man welcomes outcasts and even eats with them!
(Luke 15:2)

The Mercy of God
Is for Everyone

If I put a red tag on all the bad people and a blue
tag on all the good people (show tags) and then told
you to pick out anyone you wanted as your friends,
which ones would you pick? The good people, surely!
All your friends would have blue tags, wouldn't they?

But Jesus did not do it that way. Many of Jesus'
friends were good people—but He made friends with
the bad ones too. He never chased a sinner away, but
always made him feel at home. Remember, that is the
whole reason why our Lord came to this world—to
save sinners, to suffer and die for them, to keep them
out of hell, so they could really feel at home with Him
someday in heaven.

That's where you see our Lord today—with the
sinners.

That's the kind of story He tells today—about the
shepherd who goes after the lost sheep. The sinner is
a lost sheep, and Jesus goes after him because He loves
him—no matter how many good ones He has to leave
behind.

No matter how bad we are, God loves us. It is the
bad ones He wants to help. That is what we call the

"mercy of God." It is what we need. It is what God has plenty of.

There is a prayer we can say that tells our Good Shepherd how we feel: "Look toward me, and have pity on me, O Lord, for I am alone and afflicted; put an end to my affliction and my suffering, and take away all my sins, O my God. For Jesus' sake. Amen."

Reading: Luke 5:1-11

When Simon Peter saw what had happened, he fell on his knees before Jesus and said, "Go away from me, Lord, for I am a sinful man!" (Luke 5:8)

Be Honest with God

Once upon a time there was a little boy named David, and there was a great big giant named Goliath. Instead of a whole army, Goliath was going to fight alone for his people against the Hebrews. Whom do you think the Hebrews picked out to fight the giant? Yes sir, little David—a boy with nothing but a sling-shot like this one. But do you know what happened? With one little stone like this the boy with the sling-shot hit the big giant in the head and killed him.

Why? Why could David do that? Was it because he said, "I'm great! I'm a big shot! I can do anything"? Not at all. What David said was, "I'm fighting for God. God is on our side, and God will make us win."

Sometimes I hear people say that God never helps them. Do you know why? Because they really do not *let* God help them, because they don't give Him a chance. Because they think they can do everything by themselves. Because they think they are the "big shots" and everything depends on them.

Do you know what people like that are really saying? They are saying: "Look who I am. I'm really somebody — and God better help me. God better do just exactly what I want." *That* is the way those people "pray." But God does not answer *that* kind of prayer because prayer does not mean "telling God what to do."

St. Peter gives us the right idea in today's Bible story. When he sees that Jesus is God, he wants to get away from Him because he is just a sinner. Peter does not brag about how good he is. He admits how bad he is. David did not brag about how strong he was. He told how strong God is. Peter and David were honest with God.

If I am honest with God, I will say: "The Lord is my Light and my Salvation; whom should I fear? The Lord is my life's Refuge; of whom should I be afraid? — Because of the glory of Your name, O Lord, deliver us — O Lord, my Rock, my Fortress, my Deliverer." That is what I will say about God, if I am honest. And what I will say about myself, if I am honest, is: "Go away from me, Lord for I am a sinful man!" And the Lord will answer: "Whoever comes to Me, I will not cast out."

The Lord is my Savior; He is my strong Fortress. My God is my protection, and I am safe with Him. (Psalm 18:2)

God Is Our Strength

When you go outdoors, you see dirt and rocks, plants and trees. Of all those things, what is the strongest? Trees are pretty strong, but a big wind can blow them over. Some plants are pretty tough, but they dry up and blow away. The dirt can hold up a big building, but a flood can wash the dirt away and the building will fall. But if you really want something strong, you will take a great big rock which nothing can move.

The Word of God tells us today that our Lord is like a rock. You know that every little wind and rain won't blow or wash the rock away! We can count on the rock to be there when we want it. And we can count on our Lord to be there when we want Him too. He is strong and solid like a rock, so we can always depend on Him.

Think of the story of Peter and some of the other apostles fishing all night and not catching a thing. Then our Lord came along and told them they would catch some fish if they put their nets back in the water. They didn't believe Him, but they threw the nets into the lake anyway. And what happened? They caught so many fish they didn't know what to do with all of them. That showed the apostles that they could count on our Lord whenever He said something. It showed that He is as "solid as a rock." It showed that He is strong enough to take care of things.

Our Lord is strong enough to take care of us too. *We* can count on Him too, because He is still as solid as a rock. No matter what anyone else thinks or says or does, our Lord will never let us down.

Some people complain that their families don't care about them, nobody wants them or writes them. Others think that those in charge of them are unfair. And lots of times other boys and girls are mean to them. All these things make us feel bad. But there is something that can always make us feel good. That is when you know and can say:

> The Lord is my Light and my Salvation;
> Whom should I fear?
> The Lord is my life's Refuge;
> Of whom should I be afraid?
> My foes and my enemies
> Themselves stumble and fall.
> Though an army encamp against me
> My heart will not fear.

Reading: Matthew 5:20-24

Go at once to make peace with your brother; then come back and offer your gift to God. (Matthew 5:24)

To Love God Means to Love His People

In this hand I have a lovely present for your father on his birthday. In the other hand I have a big club. First, I am going to give the present to your father to show how much I like him. Then I am going to beat you and all your brothers and sisters with the club. What do you think of that? Do you think my present would make your father happy? Do you think I really love your father if I beat up his children?

Right now all of us have a beautiful gift ready to give our heavenly Father. All of us together are going to give our Father in heaven our worship and honor. And along with our nice words and thanks we are going to give *ourselves* to God.

Are you going to turn right around then and beat up God's children? Are you going to tell our Father that you love Him one minute and then show that you hate your brothers and sisters? You know who God's children are and who your brothers and sisters are: everyone you see today or tomorrow or any day.

Every boy and girl, every man, woman, and child whom you meet, work with, play with, or live with— they are all children of our heavenly Father, and they are all our brothers and sisters because He is the Father of us all.

But do you ever beat any of them up, have you ever struck any of them? "Oh, *no!*" you say. Oh, no? Not with a club, maybe; not with a whip, perhaps. But what a lashing you have given them with your tongue! Oh, how you have whipped your brothers and sisters with words! What terrible things you have *said* to other people! How you have cursed and sworn at God's children! How many people wish that you would strike them with a club instead of with your tongue!

St. Peter tells us that anyone who wants to get to heaven "must keep his tongue from evil." And Jesus Himself says that anyone who calls another a fool is worthy of hell. And then our Lord goes on to say that God does not want our gift at the altar so long as we are not friends with anyone else. He says we have to make up with anyone we have hurt first: *"Then* come back and offer your gift to God."

Remember, it will do us no good to come here and tell God how much we love Him and then go and use that same tongue to hurt everyone else. If we really want to show our heavenly Father that we love Him, we won't curse and swear and say all sorts of terrible things to our brothers and sisters. If you love God, prove it: stop beating up His children with your tongue.

For there is no other god who can rescue like this. (Daniel 3:29; Daniel 3:96 NAB)

God Will Always Take Care of You

I wonder if you know that radar is helping all of us all the time. Radar is a great big electric eye that can "see" planes and bombs and rockets that might be sent to kill us. These big machines that our country has all over are always "watching over" us so we won't get hurt. They are "watching" day and night so that the enemy cannot get at us.

Radar does help us, but it is just a machine. Radar can't *love* us, and radar doesn't really *care* if we get hurt. It can do wonderful things, but it can't do everything. But there is something that *can* do everything for us, something that can do more than just help us, something that can really take care of us and really keep away from us anything that might hurt us. We call that something "divine providence."

Divine providence just means God's care for us. When we pray, "O God, whose ever-watchful providence rules all things," we are saying that God is *always* "watching." But He is not watching like a machine, because He is our heavenly Father who *loves* us and *cares* for us. And He is not just watching for missiles or planes or rockets. That is why we say that He rules *all* things—because He is watching over all of His people to keep *all* things away that could hurt them and to give them all the things that can help them.

God is not a machine like radar. And you and I are not machines like rockets or planes or missiles. Radar doesn't love us, and missiles don't hate us. But God does love us — and we should love God too. Divine providence means that God will take care of us. God will do His part, but we have to do our part, too, because we are not just machines. We can *do* what God wants or *not* do what He wants.

So St. Paul tells us that we should follow Jesus and not be "slaves" to sin. And Jesus tells us that we have to be like "healthy trees" if we are going to give good fruit. We cannot get to heaven just by saying, "Lord, Lord," but we have to do what God wants!

God is not a machine like radar. He is a loving Father who watches over us and takes care of us every minute of our lives. He wants us to be loving children who are on the watch and really care too.

Reading: Romans 8:12-17

God's Spirit joins Himself to our spirits to declare that we are God's children. (Romans 8:16)

God Is Your Father

A long time ago there was a song that everybody was singing called "You Must Have Been a Beautiful Baby." Most babies are beautiful to look at, but even when they aren't, their fathers think they are.

Today St. Paul tells us that we are children of God. You know when we were made God's children — the day we were baptized. And it doesn't matter if we were good looking or not, but that day every one of us was beautiful to God. Our heavenly Father didn't look at our faces that day; He looked at our souls. And the soul of every one of us looked beautiful to God on the day of our baptism.

You know that Baptism took the sin of Adam and Eve off our souls. Before that our souls, with original sin on them, were not nice for God to look at. We were not His children. But then Baptism made our souls clean and beautiful and gave us God as our Father. How lucky we were that day when we were made children of God.

Now sometimes children run away from their fathers or get into terrible trouble, and their fathers don't think they are so nice anymore. Maybe they get into fights and get black eyes or broken noses or have their teeth knocked out. Then they aren't such "beautiful babies" anymore.

How does your soul look to your heavenly Father today? Is it still beautiful like it was on your baptism day? Or has the devil given your soul the black eye or the broken nose of sin? Has your soul run away from God your Father by doing wrong? If it has, you can come back to Him, and your soul can be beautiful again if you confess your sins.

But I hope your soul is beautiful today and that God is still your Father. A good way for us to stay children of God is by saying the Lord's Prayer every day and meaning it. In the second part of that prayer we ask our Father to keep our souls beautiful. Think of that every time you say: "Forgive us our trespasses, as we forgive those who trespass against us. And lead us not into temptation, but deliver us from evil. Amen."

Reading: Luke 16:1-9

Turn in a complete account of your handling of my property. (Luke 16:2)

Someday We Must Make an Accounting

When you count things up and make a list of them, you make an accounting. If you tell me you had a glass of juice, a bowl of cereal, two eggs, two slices of toast, and a cup of coffee for breakfast, that is an accounting. If you were in charge of all the food in the kitchen, then you would be a steward, and you would have to make an accounting of *all* the food. You would have to show how you used everything.

That is exactly what we will all have to do when we die. We will have to show God how we used everything. Our Lord told us today's Gospel story to make us think about our judgment day—the day when we will have to make an accounting of everything we are in charge of.

What are you in charge of? Everything God gives you: your body, your eyes, ears, tongue, hands, feet; your mind, your heart, your soul; all the good things you have, food, clothes, all the things you use every day. God has given you those things to help you get to heaven, to help other people and to honor Him. The minute you die He will want to know how you used all those things. He is going to ask you to give an accounting of your stewardship. And what will you say when God asks you: How did you use your body — your eyes and ears and hands and feet? Did you do good things with them? How did you use your mind and heart—to think of Me and love Me? How did you use all the good things you had—to help others and to honor Me? Or did you use all those things to hurt others, to do wrong, to sin? Did you use your body in the wrong way—to see and hear and say and do bad things? Did you use your mind to think of bad things and your heart to hate people? Did you steal or waste or throw away the good things I gave you?

When God asks you all those questions, you will have to give an accounting of your stewardship. We call that your judgment day, because God will be your Judge. That means He will say one of two things: you can go to heaven because you believed in Me and used everything the right way; or you have to go to hell because you used things the wrong way.

I hope when you make your accounting to God, you will be able to say: "I used everything the way You wanted me to." Or that you will say: "Forgive me for the many times I used things the wrong way." Then God will say: "Good for you; come to heaven."

Reading: Luke 18:9-14

O God, have pity on me, a sinner! (Luke 18:13)

Be Honest About Yourself

How can you tell the "good guys" from the "bad guys"? Right! The "good guys" wear the white hats. (Put on a white hat.) But that is only in the movies, isn't it? I hope so, because I wear a black hat! (Put on a black hat.) And of course a *bad* fellow could wear a *white* hat too. So we cannot *really* know how good a person is by the color of the hat he wears.

Well, maybe we can tell if a person is good by what he *says*. If he says, "I am a good guy," can you be sure, can you trust him? Our Lord answers that question in the Gospel story about a fellow who goes to church and tells God how good he is. He says, "I am better than everyone else. I never do anything wrong. Everything I do is right. I'm a good guy!" But there is another fellow in church at the same time. He doesn't pat himself on the back at all. He just asks God to forgive him because he is a sinner. He does not say he is a "good guy." But God says so! God says this fellow is honest. He isn't bragging and patting himself on the back. He is the one who is really good — the one who *says* he is bad.

But how about the Pharisee? What does God think of him? Not much! The Pharisee thought too much of himself — so God does *not* think much of him. The thing that made the Pharisee bad was bragging about being good, forgetting that he was a sinner.

Our Lord told that story so we would not forget. So that we would remember that we are poor, weak sinners. He wanted us to remember that He is the One who knows how good we are and how bad we are. We don't have to brag about being good. We don't have to wear a white hat. If we are really good, God knows it — we do not have to tell Him.

And if we have sinned, if we have been bad, He will forgive us — as long as we admit it — and He will *make* us good. You see, we cannot make ourselves good by saying so, by bragging, by patting ourselves on the back, by wearing a white hat. But God can

87

make us good—if we *let* Him, if we admit we *need* Him. So let's not be a Pharisee and tell God how good we are. Let's be like the other fellow and say, "O God, have pity on me, a sinner!"

Reading: Psalm 65

God, people must praise You in Zion. (Psalm 65:1)

God Is the One

"I, I, I, I, I." Five times the Pharisee brags about himself. That is what he went to church for. But there is not a single "I" in the prayer of the publican. What a difference in the way those two fellows prayed! You see, the Pharisee was not honoring God at all. He was not really praying. He was just bragging. He might better have stayed home, because he was only honoring himself—and that is not what we should go to church for.

What we should be doing in church is saying: "To *You* we owe our hymn of praise, O God . . . ; to *You* must vows be fulfilled . . . ; to *You* I lift up my soul, O Lord! . . . to give glory to *Your* name." "You, You, You, You." "*You* are the One I must praise in church, dear Lord, not myself. This is *Your* house, not mine. I come here to honor *You,* not me."

How about that? Do you ever come to church to honor yourself, to praise yourself instead of God? I can hear every one of you saying, "Of course not! We say all the prayers and sing all the songs to *God.*" Sure we do. All the *words* we say and all the *words* we sing certainly make it sound like praise to God.

But what are we *thinking? "They* always make trouble for me; *she* got me into an argument; *he* started it."

And what does all that mean? It means that *I* never start a fight, *I* never make trouble, *I* am not like everybody else. And if that is the way we feel about it, we are really praising ourselves, not God. If that is what we are thinking, then our prayers and our songs are not filled with God, but our hearts are filled with ourselves.

If we want God in our hearts, we have to put our hearts into our prayers and our songs. If we want our hearts to be filled with Him, we have to empty ourselves out of our hearts. If we come to God's house to honor Him, it won't do any good to say and sing "You, You, You" to God when we really mean "I, I, I." If we want to praise God instead of ourselves, we will not decide how good we are. We will use the words of another prayer and say to the Lord: "From *You* let judgment come; *Your* eyes behold what is right."

Reading: Mark 7:31-37

At once the man's ears were opened, his tongue was set loose, and he began to talk without any trouble. (Mark 7:35)

Religion Is Talking with God

When I use the telephone, I have to do two things: I have to talk, and I have to listen. I have to use two things: my mouth and my ear. We say *"talking* on the telephone"; but we do not just talk—we listen too. I have to talk—otherwise the fellow on the other end would not even know I am here. And I have to listen—otherwise the other fellow might just as well not be there. If the telephone is going to do us any good, *both* of us have to talk *and* listen. We call that "conversation"—two people talking *and* listening to each other.

Would you believe that is what our religion is? Religion is a conversation between two people. Religion is God talking to us and listening to us. But there is no sense in God's talking to us if we do not listen. And there is no sense in God's listening if we are not saying anything. We have to use our mouth and our ears if we want our religion to mean anything.

That is what God said to us the day we were baptized—the same thing that He said to the deaf and dumb man He healed: "Ephphatha!" which means "Open up!" When Jesus said that to the deaf-mute, his "ears were opened, his tongue was set loose, and he began to talk without any trouble." That was a wonderful thing our Lord did for that fellow. And it was a wonderful thing God did for us at our baptism, too, when through his minister he said, "Open up!" That is when it all started: when we were made God's friend, when our religion began.

Now, if we want to keep on being God's friend, if we want to keep up our religion, we have to keep our ears and our mouths open: hearing God's Word with our ears, listening to what He tells us to do; praising God with our mouths, singing and praying to Him, telling Him we love Him, thanking Him, asking for His help, saying we are sorry.

That is real religion—a two-way conversation with God. He does speak to you in the Bible, in the Commandments, through His Son Jesus Christ, and through all those who take His place. Are you listening? He does listen to you. Are you saying anything? Or is the line *dead?*

Reading: Luke 10:23-37

You must love your neighbor as yourself. (Luke 10:27)

Love Your Neighbor as Yourself

We cannot all be Boy Scouts. (Put on Boy Scout cap.) But all of us can be Good Samaritans. Everyone has seen the picture of the Boy Scout helping a poor old lady across the street. He is doing a good deed, and that's what Boy Scouts are supposed to do — good deeds. Well, today our Lord shows us the picture of the Good Samaritan and then tells us that all of us should be Good Samaritans when He says: "Go and act like *him.*"

How did the Good Samaritan act? I suppose you could say he acted like a Boy Scout. He did a good deed. He helped a poor beaten-up fellow whom he didn't even know. He helped him because he knew he was his neighbor even though he did not know who he was. That shows us that everybody is our neighbor. And God says we have to *love* our neighbor as ourselves.

If a fellow is a Boy Scout, does that mean he has to go around hugging and kissing everybody he sees? Is that how he does his "good deeds"? Of course not! He shows that he loves his neighbor by helping him, by being kind to him — just by being *nice* to people. The Good Samaritan did the same thing. He showed that he loved the poor man who was robbed and beaten up by helping him. And that showed that he really loved God.

If God stood here in front of you right now and said, "Do you love Me?" you would say, "Yes, I do!" "Then," He would say, "be a Good Samaritan. Love your neighbor. Help everyone you can. Be kind to other boys and girls. Be nice to people. If you don't love your neighbor, you don't love Me."

Of course, God is not going to stand in front of you and ask if you love Him. But He stands other people in front of you to find out if you love Him. If you really love God, you will be a Good Samaritan by being good and kind and nice to all the people around you.

Remember, a good Boy Scout does not ask *other* people to do good deeds—*he does* the good deeds. The Good Samaritan does not wait for other people to be good to him—he tries to be good to everyone else because he loves his neighbor. That shows that he loves God.

Reading: Luke 17:11-19

Jesus! Master! Have pity on us! (Luke 17:13)

How Good God Is to Us!

Leprosy is a terrible sickness. We call the people who have leprosy lepers. Sometimes the fingers and toes, the hands and feet of lepers rot right off their bodies. Sometimes they lose their ears or their noses. It is hard to stop leprosy, and most lepers die with this awful sickness.

If you saw a leper, you would surely feel very sorry for him. One day Jesus saw 10 of these people. And that is what they asked our Lord to do—to feel sorry for them and to help them. They said, "Jesus! Master! Have pity on us!" No medicine could stop their sickness; no doctor could keep the leprosy from killing them. But God could. Jesus could heal them because He is God. Our Lord could take their leprosy away because God can do anything. All the lepers did was to ask Jesus for help. Then they did what He told them to do and right away they were cured, their leprosy was gone and they were lepers no more! They asked for pity, for mercy, for help—and they got it because Jesus loved them.

None of us has ever had leprosy—and I surely hope we never will. But we all have lots of other troubles. One of our biggest troubles is even worse than leprosy: it is the terrible sickness of our souls which we call sin. We are not lepers, but we are all sinners. And like the lepers in the story, we ask Jesus to have pity on us too. Every time we worship together, we say, "Lord, have mercy; Christ, have mercy; Lord, have mercy." We are asking our Lord to help us, just as the lepers did. And our Lord does help, just as He helped the lepers—because He loves us.

How good God was to those poor suffering men! And how good He has been to us! In Baptism He takes away the leprosy of our souls. In Holy Communion He feeds our souls to keep them well, and in His Word He gives us grace and help and strength. Every time we meet in church we ask God to be sorry for us and help us. And Jesus Himself comes to give us the help we need in all our troubles.

The lepers asked Jesus for help and then did what He told them. That is all we have to do too. Every time we say, "Lord, have mercy; Christ, have mercy," we are asking for help. Let us be sure we really mean it. Then let us be sure to do what God wants, and He will surely help us.

Reading: Matthew 6:24-34

Which one of you can live a few years more by worrying about it? (Matthew 6:27)

Stop Worrying!

Are you a "Calamity Jane" or a "Gloomy Gus"? Are you a "worry wart" or a "sad sack"? Do you fuss and fret and stew? Is everything dark and dismal and dreary?

If that's the way things are with you, then "look at the birds in the sky" and "learn a lesson from the way the wild flowers grow." The birds never worry about their food; the flowers are not all bothered about their clothes. But who eats better than the birds, and who looks better than the flowers? So, "Stop worrying," our Lord says. If God takes care of the birds and the flowers, He will surely take care of you.

That is what I say to people sometimes: What are you worrying about? You get enough to eat, you have a place to sleep and clothes to wear. You have movies and television and baseball. You have games and picnics. You have someone to take care of you and nurses and doctors to keep you well. You have a roof when it rains, heat when it snows, medicine when you are sick. *What* are you worrying about?

Are you worrying about getting to heaven, about being good, about pleasing God, about keeping away from sin? Are you worrying about helping other people, about how nice you can be to someone else, about how much good you can do? You can bet you are not worrying about your soul, but your body—worrying about where you are or whom you are with or who cares about you or what people say to you.

And that is where we are wrong, St. Paul tells us. He says we should "act according to the spirit." The things of God, the things of our soul are the ones that really matter. The things of our body will always be taken care of, if we will only pay attention to the things of our spirit. Jesus Himself said that. He told us that God knows we need food and clothes and many other things. All we have to do is make sure that we follow Him and belong in His kingdom—then God will see that everything else is taken care of for us, just as He does for the birds in the sky and the lilies in the field. So, "Stop worrying."

Reading: Luke 7:11-16

"A great prophet has appeared among us!" and, "God has come to save His people!" (Luke 7:16)

God Is Always with You

Are you afraid of the dark? (Lights out.) Most people do not like to be alone in the dark and sometimes will whistle or sing because they are scared. Well, suppose it were dark all the time. Suppose we never had any light at all. That would really be scary, wouldn't it? And do you know what would happen if the sun stopped shining? After a while everything would be dark and dead. Nothing can live without the light of the sun.

God is like the sun in our souls. (Lights on.) His grace is the light which keeps our souls alive. If that light goes out, our souls are dark and dead with sin. And that is the darkness we should all be afraid of, because no soul can live without the light of God.

It is hard to think of what it would be like without

the sun. But the next time you are in a dark place, just think how it would be if it stayed like that. How would it be if you could never see anybody or find your way or get your food and drink? How would it be if nobody could see you or find you? Being in the dark all the time would be terrible, wouldn't it?

Well, being without God would be terrible too. It would be much worse than being without the sun. Do you know that that is just what hell is? Being without God is the worst part of hell. And it's the worst part of sin too, because sinning is putting God and His light out of our life.

But, thank God, we have the sun to light the world, and we have God Himself to light our souls and to light the way to heaven. It is awful without God. In fact, we can honestly say it is "hell" without God. But we are not without God. God is everywhere—all around us and even right *in* us, as long as we trust in Him and follow Jesus, His Son.

Remember that God is with you, thank Him for being with you, and be sure to ask Him to stay with you. Remember that sin puts God and His light out of your soul. Remember: hell is being without God. You will never go there as long as God is with you.

Reading: Ephesians 3:13-21

I ask God . . . that Christ will make His home in your hearts through faith. (Ephesians 3:16-17)

True Faith Is Honest

"On the level," "No kidding," "On the up and up," "Honest to goodness," and "Cross my heart" are all ways of saying the same thing. Do you know what it is? Yes: "I'm telling the truth—I am honest."

I wonder if our faith is on the level, if we are on the up and up with God, if we are honest about what we believe—or if we are kidding ourselves sometimes. That's the kind of people our Lord is talking to in the Bible story of Jesus curing a man's crippled hand (Luke 6:6 ff.). The phony Pharisees! "Phony" means dishonest. Phony people are people who do not tell the truth, people who are not on the level.

The Pharisees were phony because they made up a lot of their own rules. They faked their faith. They made believe they were holy. They looked holy, but they were only kidding. They were really lying. That is what Jesus tried to show them when He cured the sick man on the Lord's Day. The Pharisees said, "It is wrong to heal the sick on the Lord's Day because we must not work on that day." But making a sick man well is a good deed, and it is not wrong to do *good* on the Lord's Day. So Jesus did the healing just to show them that they were phony—they were not being honest about what they believed. Those fellows *said* they were holy and tried to *look* holy—but they were not holy because they really did not do what God wants. They were not honest.

I hope you are not phony like the Pharisees. I hope you don't say one thing and do another. You say you "believe" a lot of things. But remember we are just kidding ourselves if we say we *believe* what God says and then do not *do* what He wants.

St. Paul says he hopes Christ will live in our hearts through faith. Christ cannot live in a dishonest heart. If our faith is phony, Christ is out. Don't be a Pharisee. Be on the level with God; if you believe what He says, do what He wants.

Reading: Matthew 22:34-46

You must love the Lord your God with all your heart and with all your soul and with all your mind. (Matthew 22:37)

How Much Should You Love God?

How much does God the Father love you? Enough to send His Son to save you. How much does God the Son love you? Enough to die on the cross for you. How much does God the Holy Spirit love you? Enough to come right into you to make you holy. God loved you enough to make you and give you everything you have. God loves you enough to give you Himself. He loves you enough to give you heaven.

So—how much should you love God? God Himself has told you how much He wants you to love Him: "with all your heart, and with all your soul and with all your mind."

What does that mean? That we have to spend *all* our time just thinking about God, that we have to pray every minute and be in church all the time? Do we have to stop eating and sleeping and working and playing and do nothing but love God? Is that what God wants? Of course not.

If I tell you to keep your clothes clean, do you have to keep them in the washing machine every minute? Do you have to stop eating because you might spill something on your clothes, or stand up all the time because the chair is dirty, or not do your work because it means digging in the garden? Why, you just use a napkin when you eat, brush off the chair when it's dirty, and wear overalls or an apron when you work. Then you can go right on eating, sitting, or working and still keep your clothes clean.

Well, that's the way it is with loving God. We should love Him with our whole mind and heart and soul, but we do not have to stop eating and sleeping, working and playing to do that. We can show our love for God *by* those things. We can eat and sleep and work and play *because* God wants us to. That is the best way to love God—just by doing everything for Him because He does everything for us.

From now on, when you get up every morning try to remember to say: "Father in heaven, I give to You today all I think and do and say." That leaves just *one* thing you *can't* do: sin. And no matter what else you do, if you do it all for God you will be loving Him with all your heart, and with all your soul and with all your mind.

Reading: Psalm 46

He stops wars all over the world. (Psalm 46:9)

Pray for Peace

I am going to talk about mice and elephants today. The poor little mouse cannot do very much. The great big elephant can do many more things than the mouse because he is so big and strong. But there are a lot of things that elephants cannot do, either. Did you ever see an elephant skip rope or fly? Do you think elephants can bake cakes or write letters? Of course not! No matter how big and strong they are, there are some things they just cannot do.

You and I are like that too. There are a lot of things we cannot do at all. We can't jump over the top of this building or fly from tree to tree like a bird. Some of us can't even bake a cake or write a letter any more than an elephant or a mouse can. But if someone helps us, then maybe we could write the letter or bake the cake. When we have help, there are lots of things we can do that we could not do without help.

In our prayer today we ask God again to help us, and we say, "Without You we can do nothing to please You." We cannot do anything good, anything worthwhile without God's help. And that is why we have to ask Him for His help over and over again, remember.

You know that there is a terrible war going on. Many people are suffering and being hurt and getting killed. It would be a wonderful thing if we could stop that awful war. If we could go over there and just say "stop" and have the war over with, it would be *great*. But you know that we cannot do that any more than elephants can fly. But we do want peace, we do want the war to stop. Lots of people want peace and want the war to be over. Many are trying and trying to get peace in the world. But they cannot do it — not without God's help.

That is why we pray today: "Give peace, O Lord, to those who have hoped in You." Every day let us pray for peace. Let us hope in God and ask Him for peace because we know that we cannot stop the war by ourselves. We need His help. Please keep on asking Him for it.

So the servants went out into the streets and gathered all the people they could find, good and bad alike. (Matthew 22:10)

God Loves All People

Under this cover is a beautiful cake with candles on it. I wonder what that makes you think of. A birthday party, of course! Now, when you have a birthday party, you want all your friends to come. You want everybody you like to have a good time with you and to have some of the delicious cake. Nobody ever has a party all by himself.

Today the Word of God tells us that heaven is like a big party, a wedding feast. Heaven is *God's* party, and of course He wants all His friends to come to that party. He wants everybody He likes to have a good time with Him. And who are the ones God likes, or loves; who are His friends?

Well, you know that God loves everyone. He wants everybody in the whole world to get to heaven. Not just you and me, not just church people, not just Americans, not just white people. No, God wants black and brown and yellow people at His party; He wants men and women and children from Europe and Asia and Africa; He wants Protestants and Catholics and Jews and Mohammedans; He wants everybody to come and have a wonderful time at His wedding feast.

Now, suppose your friend has a birthday party,

but you don't know about it. You cannot go to the party if you don't know he is having it. Somebody has to tell you about the party, someone has to ask you to come to it. Otherwise you will miss it. You won't be there.

Do you know that there are many, many people who do not know about God's party? There are millions of people who have never heard of heaven, who have never even heard of God and His Son Jesus Christ. Someone has to tell them about God and heaven. Someone has to ask them to come to God's wedding feast or they will miss it. If they never hear about heaven, they won't be there.

The men and women who will tell those people about God and heaven and how to get there are missionaries. They go all over the world asking people to come to God's party. That is a big job, and they need our help. Today is (Mission Sunday) the day when we remember to help the missionaries and the millions of people who have not yet heard about God.

You know about God and heaven. You know how to get there. Please help all those other people to get there. Please pray today and every day for the missions. Here is an easy prayer you can say: "Dear God, I know about You. Thank You. Please help everyone else to know about You too."

Reading: John 4:46-53

Unless you people see signs and wonders, you do not believe. (John 4:48)

You Can Trust God

Do you know what an anchor is? It is a big heavy piece of iron that we put on the end of a rope to hold a boat still. One day this summer I went out in a little boat on a big river to do some fishing. The water in the river was flowing very fast, and I had to drop an anchor in the water to keep the boat from running away while I was fishing. Now, if I just let the anchor hang in the water or get caught in the mud or a bunch of weeds, it would not hold the boat still. But there were big rocks in the bottom of the river, and when the anchor caught on those rocks, it held the boat right where I wanted it. I knew that I could trust in those rocks to keep the anchor from slipping. I knew the anchor had something to hold on to.

Our life is like a big river, and we all have to have something to hang on to, or we will be washed away by sin and the devil. We all have to have something that we know we can trust in, so we don't go floating down the river to hell. There are bad people and bad things that rush around us like the waters of a big river sometimes. And if we don't get anchored to something, we will be swept right down the river of life and be lost.

What can we get anchored to, what can we hold on

to, what can we put our trust in? The man in today's Gospel story shows us: He put his trust in the word Jesus had spoken. He knew he could hang on to God. He knew he could hope in Him. That's what he did. He dropped his anchor right into the strong rocks of God's Word. And God helped him.

In the prayer today we say, "O Lord, You have given me hope," and in another place we say, "The eyes of all look hopefully to You, O Lord, and You give them their food." If we put our trust in God, He will always help us.

Sometimes I hear people say, "No one cares," "No one wants to help me," "Everyone is against me." That is not right! There is someone who is not against you, who does care, who will help you. Water or mud or weeds cannot hold the anchor of a boat. Rocks can. But you have to be sure to get the anchor into the rocks. When nobody else can help you, God can, but you have to put your trust in Him, you have to believe His Word. "O Lord, You have given me hope."

Reading: Matthew 22:15-21

Well, then, pay to the Emperor what belongs to him, and pay to God what belongs to God. (Matthew 22:21)

True Religion Must Make Sense

Today I have four things here: a dollar bill, a flower, a wallet, and a vase. Now I am going to put everything where it belongs. So I put the money in the vase and the flower in the wallet. Then I put the wallet on the altar and the vase in my pocket. Now, isn't that silly? Everybody knows that the money belongs in the wallet and the wallet in my pocket—and that the flower belongs in the vase on the altar.

And that is all our Lord is telling us today when He says that we should "pay to the Emperor what belongs to him, and pay to God what belongs to God." He is just telling us to use a little common sense. The emperor was the ruler, and people were supposed to pay him money. Jesus said that is all right: pay the ruler what you owe him. *But* don't forget about God — give Him what you owe Him too.

What do we "owe" to God? Well, we certainly owe Him thanks for all He does for us. We certainly owe Him love for all the love He has for us. We certainly owe Him an apology for the times we have hurt Him. We certainly owe Him an hour of worship on Sunday for all the hours He gives us all week long. If we really want to put things where they belong, we will surely give some time and thought and love to God.

Does that mean we will never give any time to sleeping and eating, to working and playing? Of course not! God Himself wants us to work and play, to eat and sleep, too. But He does not want us to sleep in church or to play when we should pray. He wants us to do the right thing at the right time.

Working and playing, eating and sleeping are all good things, but we have to use our heads and do them at the right time and in the right place. If we do all those things and forget about God, then we are pretty mixed up. Our Lord says: "You need food and sleep, you need work and play—give yourself to them. But remember: you need God too—be sure you give yourself to Him."

Reading: Psalm 103

Praise the Lord, my soul! (Psalm 103:1)

Clean Hearts *and* Hands

I have two boxes here. One is very pretty, and one is very dirty. Which one do you want? Well, let's see what is in the beautiful box—nothing. I guess nobody would want the dirty box. But look what's inside:

a beautiful gold vase! You see, the pretty box is not much good because it is empty. The dirty box is worth something, though — because of what is in it.

Do you remember Jesus telling us that dirty hands do not matter so much, as long as our hearts are clean? It is what's inside that really counts — not just what's on the outside. This beautiful vase is what really counts — not the dirty box on the outside of it.

Now, of course, we should never give someone a nice present like this in a dirty box. Everyone would much rather have the pretty present in a beautiful box. And our Lord did not mean that we should go around with dirty hands. But if it's one or the other, clean hearts are better than clean hands; beautiful gold vases are better than beautiful gold boxes. But the best thing of all is to have *both:* clean hearts *and* hands, and the nice gift *in* the nice box. There! That's the way to give a gift.

Have you noticed how we say over and over, "Praise the Lord, my *soul!*" How do we praise the Lord? With prayer and song. But remember: God does not want our songs and our prayers to come only from our lips. That would be like a beautiful empty box. What good is it? God wants us to mean what we say, to mean what we sing. He wants our praise to come from our hearts. "Praise the Lord, my *soul*" — not just my lips.

Of course we can love and honor God *just* in our hearts — without saying or singing a single thing. And that's better than shouting out a lot of songs and prayers that we don't really mean.

But remember what we all like best: the nice gift inside the nice box. Remember what God likes best: the nice praise inside our hearts *with* some nice prayers and songs on our lips. It does not matter if we have a beautiful voice or not. If we really mean in our hearts what we sing and say with our lips, then it is a beautiful gift to God in a beautiful package. So: *mean* it and then *say* it and *sing* it! "Praise the Lord, my soul!"

Reading: Mark 9:33-35

Whoever wants to be first must place himself last of all. (Mark 9:35)

The Last Shall Be First

I have six cards here which are all worth some money. But they are not all worth the same. Every one is different. Which one do you think is worth the most? Well, let's turn the first one over. It has a penny pasted on it. Now look at the back of the second one: a nickel. The third is worth a dime. The fourth a quarter; the fifth, 50 cents. But look at the last one: a whole dollar. So, you see, the last card is the best card. If you could have one of these cards, which one would you take first? The last one, of course. Now you know how the last can be first, and you see that the last can be the most important.

You do not have to be first to be important. In today's Gospel story the apostles were having a little scrap among themselves. They were arguing with one another about who was the most important. Can't you just hear them: "I know more than you do. I'm the oldest one. I'm stronger than everyone else. I'm first. I'm first. I'm first."

But what did Jesus say? "Whoever wants to be first must place himself last of all." If you put *your-self* first, you will be like this penny card—not worth very much. But when you put yourself last, then you are like the dollar card—the most important of all.

You see, nobody likes braggadocio. Nobody likes a braggart. What in the world does that mean? Well, a braggart is a fellow who brags, the fellow with all the "I's": I, I, I, I, I, the fellow who always puts himself first, who tries to make everybody believe that he is the most important of all. That's braggadocio—being full of bragging, being a braggart, thinking that you are better than everyone else, always wanting to be first.

Most people wouldn't give two cents for a braggart. Remember the first card: it isn't worth two cents, either—only one cent. Being first does not make you worth the most. Thinking you are the best does not make you the best. Who does *God* think is the best? Jesus told us: the one who puts himself *last*—like the dollar card. That's the one you like the best. Don't forget that God likes the *people* best who put themselves last too. If you want *God* to put you first, just be sure that you never put *yourself* first—you might end up not being worth very much.

Reading: Matthew 13:24-30

Let the wheat and the weeds both grow together until harvest. (Matthew 13:30)

Do Not Follow Bad Examples

Which one of these would you rather have? This one, of course, because it is a beautiful flower. The other one is just an ugly weed. But you know that both of them grew in the same ground, maybe right next to one another. The weed is not just ugly, but prickly too, and you could even be hurt by it. So I guess we could say the flower is good and the weed is bad.

Our Lord tells us today that people are that way too. Some are good and some are bad. Just like good seeds and bad seeds all planted in the same field, good and bad people are all mixed in together. Just as this flower might have grown with weeds growing right beside it, so good and bad people are side by side too.

And you remember, Jesus said the weeds should not be pulled out. That means that God leaves the bad right in with the good. It means that you will see and hear people around you doing and saying the wrong things. It means that no matter how hard *you* try to be good, there will always be others who are *not* trying to do the right thing.

How about that? What should we do? Should we give up trying to be good and go along with the bad fellows? Should we turn against those who are not behaving themselves? Should we throw out the bad ones?

Listen to what St. Paul tells us: "Bear with one another and forgive whatever . . . you may have against each other." He says that we should treat everybody with "mercy, kindness . . . [and] patience." In other words, no matter how bad anyone else is, we should be good to them.

Do we have to be bad because the fellow next to us is bad? Look at this flower. Did it turn into a weed just because there were weeds growing around it? Of course not; it's still a beautiful flower. And we can stay beautiful, too, even if there is badness around us. But we have to have help. We have to keep saying, "O Lord, watch over us with constant, loving care." Every plant needs constant, loving care to be beautiful.